C000192894

Notes to parents

This picture dictionary includes 150 first words that children are likely to encounter in their early years. Arranged alphabetically, they make a useful first dictionary or spelling book.

Picture definitions rather than written definitions are given here.

Written definitions are unnecessary at this stage because the words chosen will all be familiar to the young child. What is important is that the child begins to recognize that certain groups of words begin with the same initial sound or letter. Point to the pictures and play 'I spy'. Talk about the words on each page. Ask your child to think of some more words beginning with the same letter.

Look at the alphabet printed in 'small' letters at the beginning of the book and 'big' letters at the back. Encourage your child to learn to recognize the shape and sound of the letters. Look out for letters on street signs, on television, in magazines, books and newspapers or when you go shopping.

When your child is more familiar with the book and the order of the letters turn to the exercise at the back of the book and have fun finding specific pictures and letters.

picture
dictionary

written by Brenda Apsley

illustrated by David Mostyn

Filmset in Nelson Teaching Alphabet
by kind permission of
Thomas Nelson and Sons Ltd.

Copyright © 1989 by World International Publishing Limited.
All rights reserved.
Published in Great Britain by World International Publishing Limited.
An Egmont Company, Egmont House, P.O. Box 111, Great Ducie Street, Manchester M60 3BL.
Printed in Germany. ISBN 0 7235 2470 X
2nd Reprint

A CIP catalogue record for this book is available from the British Library

A a

acorn

aeroplane

alphabet

ambulance

ant

apple

apron

B b

ball

bat

bed

bird

boat

boy

bus

C c

cake

car

cat

chair

clock

cow

cup

D d

dad

desk

dig

dog

doll

door

duck

E e

eagle

ear

egg

elephant

engine

envelope

exit

F f

farm

fence

fish

flower

fork

frog

fruit

G g

garden

gate

girl

goat

goose

grapes

green

H h

hat

head

hedge

hen

hill

horse

house

I i

ice

ice-cream

igloo

ink

insect

iron

island

J j

jar

jeans

jeep

jelly

jigsaw

jug

jumper

K k

kangaroo

kettle

key

king

kitchen

kite

kitten

L l

ladder

lamb

leaf

letter

lion

log

lorry

M m

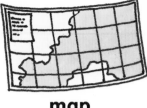

map

medal

milk

monkey

moon

mouse

mum

N n

nail

nest

newspaper

night

nose

numbers

nurse

O o

octopus

oil

onion

orange

ostrich

oven

owl

P p

paints

panda

pencil

picture

pig

potato

puppy

Q q

quarter

queen

quilt

R r

rabbit

red

ring

S s

sand

sea

shop

sink

sock

star

sun

T t

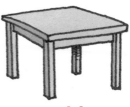

table

teddy bear

television

tooth

toys

train

tree

U u

umbrella

underwear

unicorn

V v

vase

vegetables

violin

W w

water

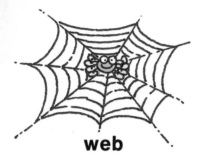
web

whale

window

wool

X x

x-ray

Y y

yacht

yellow

yo-yo

Z z

zebra

zip

zoo

These pictures are all in the book somewhere. But you have to find them!

Find each picture in turn, then read the word that belongs to it. What letter does each word begin with?

the letters of the alphabet

A B C

H I J K

O P Q

U V W